STRANGE MATTERS

M.R. Graham

More by M.R. Graham

The Liminality Series
The Medium
The Mora
The Mage
The Martyr (Coming Soon)

In the Shadow of the Mountains
The Wailing

The Adventures of Morrigan Holmes
No Cage for a Crow
The Death of a Swan (Coming Soon)

The Van Helsing Legacy
We Shall Not Sleep
Dark and Hungry Graves (Coming Soon)

Poetry
Versos, or, The Things a Woman Learns on the Banks
of the Great River
Papalotes: Songs of Texas
Strange Matters

Also
The Truth of the Matter
Proof: A Short Tale of the Undead

Table of Contents

Left Brain

I am a case study in creation,
deconstructing souls even as my larynx forms
songs.
What is happening up there where the intellect
resides,
between synapse and stardust?
And where does it go when the sparks die?

coelacanth

We crawled from the water
like the first legged creatures,
young vertebrates gasping in the sharp air.
Yearning for flight,
we hugged the ground fearfully
and thrust fingers into the raw soil,
mimicking the roots all around us,
but we did not grow.

Darkness stroked the moon-streaked sky,
where stars and rain fell as one.
We saw none of this with our blind cavern eyes,
but we felt the lights sparkle against our upturned
faces,
and we swore one day, we would see.

Sing

Sing, my soul, from high above
this brittle world of paste and foam,
insubstantial, frail, and cold.

I am but a wisp, myself,
but I make my own light,
for I am sparks,
and stars,
and candle flames,
and dreams.

warm gold

The colour of bourbon
   in crystal tumbler
taste of nothing on my lips
awareness of the skin
   beneath my eyes
candle flame
gold and caramel
smell of honey
rippled surface of jasmine tea

inner phosphorescence.

thankfully

I can feel in my veins
life thrumming
a quiet tune with the taste
of Joplin

There is sun outside
and the soles of my feet
grow into the ground

Breath comes fast
then slow
someday stops
when I shall rest

Green leaves and brown
mockingbird
dove-gentle

To be in this world
this very world
how strange and wonderful
to be.

Survive

And I will run
until my frictive bones
smolder with the heat of determination,
sliding past myself

-again-

-again-

until I self-ignite.

Clear eyes are a blessing
when the mists are black and rancid.
I would rather burn
than drown.

Girl of Flesh

I am not so human as you think,
a girl of flesh with blood to bleed.
Credit me with greater subtlety;
can flesh approach the winter and the night?
touch the stars and breathe their misty chill?
stand before the ire of men?

My flesh is lightning, hot and sharp.
My blood is the thunder.
Cut me and hear my fury roar volcanic.
I am not so human as you think,
built as I am of word and time.

Nothing

I used to be lightning.
Power surged beneath my skin,
    and in the silence, I heard myself thrum.

I used to be fire.
I burned bright inside, stellar lungs,
    and in the cold, I sang myself warm.

Still and dark.
My stone sinews crack.

I am vacuum, deep void of space.
Asteroid dust, floating.
Aimless.
Impotent.
I freeze.

Precipice

Lover,
When our wings intertwined
and I fell into your music –
(It flowed like a trance and
dampened my skin with droplets, pianissimo) –
I could have lost myself
in your sonata storm
and let my chitinous scales wash away.

Lover,
I knew even then
those strings held you bound
in ways I never could.

Fortunato's Prayer

Lure me in with silk and gold,
beaded velvet, satin threads
drawn across lips still red with wine.

Draw me down beneath the world
into some secret, wanton lair
while Carnival still beats within our veins.

Wall me up behind the dark
and leave me with my silver chains
to think on wiles byzantine,

Montresor's bleak design.

Pirate Moon

A bloody moon rose, hungry, through the mist
to wash his crimson glow across the waves
and froth the surging whitecaps with the kiss
that sent ten thousand sailors to their graves.

Beneath that vicious moon, a sail was set –
as was the fate of some poor, hapless crew
oblivious to the impending threat
that drifted ever closer through the blue.

The moon smiled sweetly, bathing naked steel,
as cannon shuddered through the velvet night
to rend the sodden trader, hull and keel
and put an end to her frenetic flight.

The captain's grin shone redder than his sword
As he o'ersaw the booty brought aboard.

Vampire

I never could refuse a drop of red
to wash down evenings thick with stress and strife
-
I never did believe that love is dead,
but love can never quench my thirst for life.
Warm lips are fine, and roving, needy hands;
there's satisfaction in a single night.
I never cared much, though, for one-night stands,
when hundreds of forevers hover right
beneath your skin. Before the sun appears,
I'll hush your frantic heart and drink your fears.

Owl Woman

Night-eyes are watching me,
candles in the dark,
a refractory guardian on guileless wings.
Is that the click of pearls I hear,
or enameled talons, a hungry beak?
When she primps and preens,
I sometimes find
feathers
in her hair,
sleek pinions under her dress.

Good morning, twilight lady.

Apocalypse Ball

If silk could melt
to drip down arms and goosebumped legs
in scarlet rivers, serpentine,
it seems only right
that the sky should burn as well.
Like roses heaped upon a stage,
cloaked in tumultuous applause,
the end will fall in exultation.
Shall we stand upon the shore
and taste the salt upon our lips,
basking in the last breezes
before the Breaking?
These last days are a ball,
a promenade of bliss,
sublime devastation,
a eulogy of memory.
Shiva, ever the gentleman,
asks for one last dance.

On Ayala

Beneath the trees, betwixt the stately pines,
the Lady and her beastly Lord see all.
The wealdkin loose their tongues and raise their
heads
to lift the forest heart with secret songs.
And in their verdant halls, the twain hold court,
attended by the eagle, fox, and hart,
accepting tribute, as is their just due.
A force of heroes, sleeping at their feet,
lie cold and white, until the time shall come
to rise again and fly beyond the mists
in service to the King Returned. But now
a time more yet must pass before they wake,
and life shall slumber still within their veins
until the Lord and Lady call them back
to take their place in wicked earth again.
Then those twain shall rule the city and the wold,
and stone and steel and murder be laid low,
for where the gods of Life should choose to tread,
no grief can fall nor human psyche know
the sting of death. The night will be here soon
when maid and beast will dance beneath the moon.

Wanderer

My world dissolves into autumn,
the shade and the fire draped about my throat
like so many jewels.
I met the mist as an old lover,
let the dew paint my lips
with the scent of harvest.
In a white memory, you are still walking away,
down that same road.
Your hair was shining like the fall.
Your shape in the fog beckons;
ghost or vision, I care not.
I lose myself.

The Dogs of War

And Caesar's spirit, ranging for revenge,
with Ate by his side come hot from hell
shall in these confines with a monarch's voice
cry 'Havoc!' and let slip the dogs of war;
that this foul deed shall smell above the earth
with carrion men, groaning for burial.

They said the fields ran with ink,
but real men bleed black on white,
and young men bleed green,
and women do not bleed at all.
They said vengeance was a worthy cause.

The dogs of war left teeth-marks in their throats.
Caesar gurgled and died, but his spirit was mute.
Havoc ensued without his order,
and the stones of Rome boiled and flowed
in rivers hot as Ate's eyes.

They tore the road-signs down
and salted the scorched earth.
Carthago delenda est - a thousand years ago.
The temples burned and the virgins took up
swords.

A carrion man, a crow man, erupts from the earth
to eat the flesh of generals
and gnaw on Caesar's bones.
Even buried, he does not sleep.

The Bard had cunning, but no sight.

He wrote in tragedy as tragedy,
that which in truth was holocaust,
the conflagration of ancient words.

And throats groan.
And teeth bite.
And Caesar is dead,
dead as cinderblock walls.

To the Ghosts of Glen Coe

Sleep, you brave, you innocent,
you warriors and women strong.
Dread William's days are now all spent,
and memory is long.

On the glen, the snow lies deep,
as once it lay those years ago,
the night it witnessed traitors creep
on sleeping Invercoe.

Great MacIain ope'd his doors
to Campbells shiv'ring in the night.
He had grown tired of English wars
and looked not for a fight.

Sleep, you brave, you innocent,
you warriors and women strong.
Dread William's days are now all spent,
and memory is long.

Screams of children drowned the storm
when Campbell blades came slicing down
on bloody tartan, rent and torn,
all for a foreign crown.

Donald blood can turn to ice,
though noble hearts beat hot and fierce –
a man, a frozen sacrifice –
a mother's dying tears.

Sleep, you brave, you innocent,
you warriors and women strong.
Dread William's days are now all spent,
and memory is long.

Under trust you met your ends;
within your walls they laid you low.
The men you welcomed as your friends
left blood upon the snow.

Seventy and eight you were,
the martyrs of that winter night,
left to char in homes afire
or cut down in your flight.

Still, the gloaming holds you here,
when February nights are still,
the skirl of Donald pipes rings clear
and echoes in the rill.

Sleep, you brave, you innocent,
you warriors and women strong.
Dread William's days are now all spent,
and memory is long,
yes, memory is long.

InsertTitle_1

We, the petty,
we, the bourgeois,
poring over mirrors of reflected, collected verse,
only we could drown
in the shallow pools of our own desires.
Self-worth and efficacy distort, distend,
dilate.
Our longing sighs inflate
gauzy bladders, diaphanous,
and we fancy them substantial because they are
large -
(We say much the same of our philanthropy.)
- seeking no synonyms,
though "bloated" comes to mind.

A pseudonym can shelter
the sodden intellect, emaciated,
denigrated by false modesties.
How quaint.
How deep, the brainy poet
who breathes his own despite
behind alabaster walls,
sherry perched atop whalebone fingers,
sloshing like the contents of his skull.
Poseur.

The Sisters

i
Two sisters sat on the edge of a cliff –
and one was old, and one was young
and their mother was not yet born.
They watched the sea below their feet.

The waves chewed at the rocks
as they had built the cliff through ages,
and green weeds flowed with the tide
like the sisters' hair on the wind.

The sisters sat for many hours,
their fingers twined with strands of yellow grass,
their eyes like chips of ocean glass,
fixed on the far horizon.

Without a word, they sang to each other
and rivalled and warred in silence
as siblings do
without a real reason to fight.

And the grass became a violin
beneath the elder's hands.
Her pizzicato challenge lost itself
somewhere between Dover and Calais.

The younger never heard it,
trapped as she was in a book
of her own invention
with half a reality against its spine.

So they stayed, forevers in the hours,
inside an opal fog, so thick they could see
everything
except one another,
but no eyes were needed for that.

ii
Two sisters sat on the edge of a cliff –
and one was old, and one was young
and their mother was not yet born.
They watched the sea below their feet.

Conjugating the tones of fortune,
it slipped their minds to turn around
and check on the declensions.
Amo amas amat, mittimus mittitis mittunt

Under the angles of the clouds
but above the drop of the cliff, something got
stuck,
and two sisters sat alone
amidst the swarms of tourists.

Diutissime, something something
and a subjunctive of some sort, yes?
But after a moment, they lost the beat
and leaned against one another's shoulders for
protection.

iii
Three sisters sat on the edge of a cliff –
and one was old, and one was young
and the other was not yet born.

They watched the sea below their feet.

And the endless seas incarnadine
watched right back.

The Hole You Left

A bizarre kind of high
is the blue depth of pain,
like the pressure in your lungs
from the clear nitrous mask
when they tear out your teeth
and you laugh through the holes
in a bruised, splintered jaw
for the tickles in your brain
and the bubbles in your blood
like a flute of champagne
at a wedding...

And the gaps left behind
in a moth-eaten soul –
like a sheet on a car
that's been out in the yard
for twenty years or so,
like a veil on a virgin
or a shroud on a corpse,
maybe coming, maybe going,
never staying very long,
like a Hallowe'en ghost –
but I digress...

No, the gaps left behind
in that sandblasted soul –
can be filled by delusion,
'til it runs out your eyes
and it soaks through your gut
with a mean, vengeful glee –
are the things you hold tightest,

for the one who has gone
is now best remembered
by the shape of the shadow
of the pale silhouette
of the hole where they once filled your heart...

Feather

Becoming light,
in truth I am falling,
slow and soft like motes of dust.
Downward still,
I sometimes think I am rain,
and I know the earth lies somewhere below.

Gilt

As I await the final gilding of the leaves
in the crown of the oak, life rises up around me,
warm, in shades of amber. Fury of peace
and stillness of motion together encircle a frail
humanity.
The darkness that falls now is gentle,
like a friend's touch, or morning tea,
and quells the darkness behind me.
There is no cause for fear.

14 Jan

Softly, softly, beautiful girl.
The dark is warm and deep,
a cocoon of heartbeats and history.
Sleep now and emerge in glory.

Reprieve

So sorrow, weary, shut her eyes in sleep,
and for a time will trouble me no more.
Again in time I must abide to weep,
but now I tiptoe past her unshut door,
my comforts silent, lest the tyrant wake,
and unto stormless joy myself betake.

Babel

I have lost the gift of tongues,
or perhaps I never knew how to speak at all.

In dreams, I have seen the tower crumbling
and felt my throat closed against my fellow
humans,
my voice crumbling, too,

never to be heard again.

Lovecraft

A solemn spire, spearing, soaring, -
stabbing.
This I saw through sleeping eyes.
Saw, perceived, yet did not know
and could not understand.
Lit by sullen stars, sagging
in a sodden sky,
it rose through roiling mist, alone
on an unseen plane,
and sank again, serene,
into the depths of my mind.

Animal

I am the wilderness
the rage and the teeth,
the tameless sea,
the nameless storm.
I am claws and eyes aglow,
the strange silences
beyond the circle of firelight.
Watch,
and love,
and fear,
for I am Wild.

Wordsmith

They wrote in ink the shade of blood,
and humans drank their words,
knowing not the poison they imbibed.
Blood, ink, gall.
Words flow into silence, into endings.
Endings sleep like death.
They wrote "The End"
and slept.

Inception

By the light of an oil-barrel fire, an idea takes
form.
In the back of a mind, psychic and gamine, trains
of
thought meet at a dirt-road intersection, four-way
stop, rays charge to intercept, travelling at exactly
three-quarters of the speed of light. The wide-eyed
ingenue with the lemon-puckered mouth cannot
but
stare in wonder (wander) from behind a blast
screen.

Orange and red, the autumn-coloured realisation
lacks a mushroom cloud or any higher pennant to
announce its nativity. The bright flash sucks back
with the noise of a deflating bladder – splat – to
hold itself secure in the knowledge of its own
singularity. There are no shepherds nearby to hear
ghost particles proclaiming peace in the instants
before their inevitable, startling annihilation.

Ain't no trouble, Bubba, is all the advice offered
by
the wrecker captain in the tall billed cap. Only
thing is,
ain't no way I can get out before the event horizon
finds-

Nobody said a word, only raised antiquated
sunglasses

to ward off the glare. If NASA had been in charge of

this operation, we might have stood a chance, but ideas

eat more fuel than a single mammal can safely secrete.

It has a hungry mouth, this one, and a warning sticker

too large even for the State of California. I told them

to retain the receipt until after Christmas had gone.

Proclaim

Beneath the spangled, auburn sky,
the silence of cathedrals swells where once
the vulgar shouts held sway, the profane
and the irreverent, the raucous, the bold.

A hush grows ever deeper in the mouths
and in the ears of the sharp-toothed
sycophant and the frog-mouthed boor,
and for once, this once, they listen.

A raffia-soled sandal shushes through the gloom,
bearing in bent shoulders beneath raglan sleeves
and a heavy brow. A confessor stands ready
in every alcove, in every ribs-bare window.

Ready are they to receive those who come.
In robes as black as searching pupils they have
waited
for the sinner-supplicant to kneel amidst the
standing
and proclaim the new amidst the old --

in a mighty voice of silence. An army of
philosophers
can outgrow the need for shouting. Someday
their gaping mouths will heal and they will learn
the comfort of a prayer in the heart.

Even now, their clamorous psalms die
on their frigid lips, and sober thought lifts

a curious glance: "Come, let us be silent. Did you know
there are other voices than ours?"

If awe could be transmitted, like a germ or radio wave,
the whole world would be silent and our vestigial mouths
would know only
how to kiss.

Urban Nomad

She treks through solemn jungles of glass and
smoke with sand in her hair and sapphires in her
pockets, bedecked in bangles and charms. The
want
of sun has made her hard; cement and steel have
scarred her feet. Blistered hands can weave wild
tales; cracked lips are made for smiling. Even in
the grey, she can always find a place to worship.

There is a roadside diner that smells of fresh coffee
and old grease and tastes like a billion miles of
empty sky. The cracked linoleum still remembers
the old Route 66, crumbs of asphalt under the
tables,
ostrich-leather boots, and a gut-buster Friday
special.

How many colours can a skyscraped nomad hold
in
her cupped hands?

Failed Words

I wrote a poem for you
full of complicated metaphor
and abstract terms
philosophising on beauty and love
and the relationship between
an ocean wave and the curve of your eyelashes
or your flawless brow and the sound of silk on
wood
rather like the Song of Solomon.
But then I remembered your heart
and the words fell away
one by one and laid you bare
inside my mind
where all of my imperfect words cannot sully you
and your beautiful imperfections.
So the only words now left are –
All I can say now is –
Thank you for being.

Socialite

There was always a certain bitterness in her
extravagance,
in the curve of her fingers around the stem of a
champagne flute,
or the wet, visceral slither of her endless strings of
pearls over sun-bitten shoulders.

Her small-talk was ruinous, but they always
laughed and called her witty
and came back again and again for more, even
when her words mauled them.

Those cynical galas seemed to drag on for years,
with crowds of dancers turning mechanically to
tinned tunes,
the ones her society friends approved.

I think now it was all carefully staged, her
prolonged suicide,
all masked with prodigal glamour, wine and
sparkle.

Her worshipers were left agog at the banality of the
final act.
Twenty storeys down, it was discovered her
diamonds were all paste.

Incantation

Somnus
Sleep descends like a bridal veil,
gossamer, pale, and translucent,
like the vine-vein traced eyelids,
trimmed in dark lace, falling.

Somnium
Dreams are solid, all too real
to those who dream with open eyes.
I dreamed a single, silent flame,
close enough to warm the glossy night.

Sonor
Whisper, or you'll wake the sleeper
and brush away the drifting dreams,
break them like filaments of silk
with that errant vibration.

Sophia
I can believe what I see in sleep,
the wisdom of the silence,
breathing in echoes of echoes of echoes:
"Be still."

Sors
Like the fall of dice, or cards drawn,
each random synapse fires
with a certain aim, a touch,
a nightly glow of prophecy.

Bedtime Story

Eyes are closed for evening
as the stories open,
dreams unfurling like night lilies.
I have breathed their perfume
and am ready to sleep.

Long Night

The sun was late today,
so late, I thought she might have forgot
to set her alarm.
The stars grew concerned,
and the night breezes whispered.
But it turns out she was just sleeping in.

The Rain Came

It stampeded like buffalo across the plains
and I heard hooves in the sky
striking fire from flint
and shaking loose the water of the heavens
with terrible fury
and roaring of fearsome throats

until we waded and struggled
in darkness through the flood below.

Flames of Autumn

The flames of Autumn sear the sullen sky
with ruby, rose, carnelian, and wine–
the heady draught which slips to sparkling night,
where may the gauds of ghosts and grims
combine.

Boreal

The mists of winter creep into my bones
a slow hibernal draught of frosty sleep
refracting shades of crystal, rainbow tones
and drawing dewy dreamers deep and deep.

Like icy ferns unfurling o'er my skin,
the twilight rest of Boreas begin.

Home for Christmas

An excelling beauty,
the hedgerows, snow-cloaked
beneath a sky that never ends,
exulting in all the hues of diamond.

Frost is a thing eternal:
in the effervescent air,
even time is frozen.

And I wonder how I ever left,
and when I shall come home.

To a Somewhere-Lover

Please introduce me to myself.
When I pass you in some hall,
let our eyes meet.
And when you see me in the street,
let me know you.
Tell me how I've waited,
and tell me how I take my tea
in the white afternoons.
Tell me how I read in the near-dark,
listening to false rain.
Describe my mornings,
mocking-bird wings and the smell of my coffee.
List my books –
the ones beside the bed
and the ones I keep between my lips.
Tell me that you heard the words I scratched
into the tops of picnic tables
and the lines I drew across time.
Tell me, love, for you have been here all along.

I carried you in my heart.

Not Birdie to You

Don't compare her to a songbird
when she is plover-sharp and raven-clever
with falcon eyes and eagle pride
and talons never meant to perch on fingers

Eyes Closed

Breaths of cool autumn on my skin,
and the smell of younger days:
cranberry, pumpkin,
spice I cannot at present name.

The house creaks with the wind outside.
I am present, wholly so.
A rare occurrence, this.
Flannel, dry heat, smooth candle wax.

Here and now.

About M.R. Graham

M.R. Graham is a native Texan who traces strong cultural roots back to Scotland, Poland, England, and Germany. A mild-mannered PhD student during the day, Graham transforms at night into a raging Holmesian loremaster and rabid novelist.

Though passionate about all scholarship and academia, Graham's training and true love lies with anthropology, particularly the archaeological branch.

Visit M.R. Graham at quiestinliteris.com or connect at facebook.com/authormrgraham.

Special thanks to my dear patrons.

You can support the author and receive early access and special extras by contributing on Patreon at patreon.com/mrgraham.

www.ingramcontent.com/pod-product-compliance
Lightning Source LLC
Chambersburg PA
CBHW021135020426
42331CB00005B/785